RENOIR
BY

Renoir

KNOPF
75 YEARS·OF·PUBLISHING

This is a Borzoi Book
Published by Alfred A. Knopf, Inc.

Introduction Text Copyright © 1990 by Rachel Barnes

Originally published in Great Britain by
Webb & Bower (Publishers) Limited, Exeter, Devon

Series devised by Nicky Bird

Designed by Vic Giolitto

Library of Congress Cataloging-in-Publication Data
Barnes, Rachel.
    Artists by themselves. Renoir/Rachel Barnes. — 1st American ed.
      p. cm.
    "Originally published in Great Britain by Webb & Bower
(Publishers) Limited, Exeter"—T.p. verso.
    ISBN 0-394-58908-4 : $16.95
    1. Renoir, Auguste. 1841–1919 — Sources. 2. Painting — Themes.
motives. I. Title.
ND553.R45B33 1990
759.4 — dc20
                              90–52731
                                 CIP

Manufactured in Italy
First American Edition

CONTENTS

Introduction 6

Renoir by Renoir 18

Chronology 78

Acknowledgements 80

INTRODUCTION

One of Pierre-Auguste Renoir's very last utterances as an old man was characteristically modest: 'I think I'm at last beginning to understand something about it,' he said, referring, of course, to his life's passion – his painting. Today, Renoir is one of the best known and loved of all painters. He is reproduced ubiquitously and his effortless charm, his sunbathed vision of human life, ever joyful and optimistic, have appealed over time to connoisseurs and the more casual observer alike.

The immediate surface charm and intense sensuality of his painting, however, give a false impression of the personality of the artist. Renoir has frequently been depicted as an affable and stable character, exuding as much warmth and sense of well-being as his famous paintings. Yet closer examination of his writings and recorded speech suggests a number of paradoxes and contradictions, and a picture begins to emerge of a man who was often anxious and unsettled, frequently besieged by self-doubt over his direction as a painter, and at times insecure about his working class origins, particularly as he began increasingly to mix with the bourgeoisie.

Renoir's father was a tailor who moved from Limoges to Paris when Renoir was three. Léonard Renoir recognised the artistic gifts of Pierre, his sixth child, but was anxious to channel them into a sensible artisan's occupation, so he obtained a job for him as a decorator in the firm of Levy Frères, porcelain manufacturers in the Rue du Temple. Here, Renoir learned to imitate Fragonard and Boucher, the great Rococo painters of the eighteenth century, who remained his heroes throughout his career. Using fluid, delicate

Returning from the Fields, 1886, Document Archives Durand-Ruel

colour on the smooth porcelain surface, Renoir developed a technique which later on was to give him his extraordinarily fluent ability to apply paint on canvas.

The story of Renoir's early apprenticeship in Charles Gleyre's studio in Paris in the early 1860s is well known, as is the legendary tale of the master's conversation with his young pupil. 'Doubtless you paint for your own amusement?' Gleyre asked him, to which Renoir replied, 'Yes, I assure you if it didn't amuse me, I wouldn't do it.' The apprenticeship to Gleyre, however, was less important to Renoir than his meeting there with three other young artists, Claude Monet, Alfred Sisley and Jean Frederic Bazille. With Monet in particular, he struck up a deep friendship and developed a sympathetic artistic exchange which was to become the basis of the whole Impressionist movement.

In the summer of 1869 the two painters worked together at La Grenouillère, on the river Seine. Their shared fascination with working in the open air and studying the transient effects of light, atmosphere and weather conditions on the surface of the water produced the first revolutionary Impressionist works. The pointillist technique of applying the paint in dots and dashes also evolved at this time. The movement was not actually labelled 'Impressionist', however, until their first group exhibition in 1874, when the critic Louis Leroy recoiled in horror on seeing Monet's painting of 1872 entitled 'Impression, Sunrise', feeling it to be not a painting at all but, as its title might suggest, merely an impression.

These early paintings were scorned and derided by both critics and public, and it was to be another decade before their revolutionary approach to painting had become sufficiently acceptable to earn any of the artists in the group a living. Renoir and Monet, in particular, had to endure considerable poverty in these early years.

By the time of the first exhibition in 1874 a number of other artists had joined the group, amongst them Sisley, Pissarro, Cézanne, Degas, Guillaumin, Boudin and Berthe Morisot: between this first exhibition and the last, in 1886, the group were to hold eight altogether. Renoir's own application of Impressionist principles, though, was completely original. Unlike the overriding preoccupation of Monet, Pissarro and Sisley with nature and landscape, Renoir was always predominantly a painter of the human form – even his landscapes usually focused on the activity of the figures in them.

Portrait of Madame Renoir, c.1885, Philadelphia Museum of Art: W. P. Wilstach Collection

Landscape at Beaulieu, 1893, The Fine Arts Museum of San Francisco, Mildred Anna Williams Collection

Many of the quotations in this book show that although Renoir's painting came naturally to him, he frequently agonized over his work. After fourteen years of producing brilliant canvases in the Impressionist style, he suffered a complete crisis of confidence. Later he wrote of this time: 'About 1883, a kind of crisis occurred in my work. I had gone to the end of Impressionism and I was reaching the conclusion that I didn't know how either to paint or to draw. In a word, I was at a dead end.'

For Renoir, this was a total *volte-face*: having spent the earlier part of his career rejecting traditional artistic values, he spent most

Young Girl with a Rose, 1886, Document Archives Durand-Ruel

of the 1880s rediscovering classicism through Ingres and the artists of the Renaissance, teaching himself to paint and draw in the manner he had previously dismissed. 'Les Parapluies', painted over the first few years of the 1880s, is an intriguing half-way mark, the bourgeois family on the right hand side of the painting showing the decorative, pointillist technique whilst the rest of the canvas, painted a little later, shows a linear, classically influenced technique. Eventually, by the 1890s, Renoir did return to his former Impressionist manner, and in his later years pushed forward his exploration of colour and light on the human form until it reached the ultimate expression of sensuality in his last series, 'The Bathers'.

Around 1880 Renoir met his future wife, Aline Charigot, a dressmaker working in Paris. He first painted her in his 'Luncheon of the Boating Party' of 1880 (see p 43) looking sweet and beguiling as she strokes the little dog amidst the general festivities. But Renoir's attitude to women was ambiguous. He once told his son Jean, 'I can only tolerate women in my home,' later explaining to him. 'I love women ... they doubt nothing. With them the world becomes something very simple. They give everything its correct value and well realize that their laundry is as important as the constitution of the German Empire. Near them one feels reassured.' Yet on other occasions he made more derogatory comments, indicating that for him women could never provide companionship. He wrote to his friend Gallimard in 1900, 'I'm fine, but I need a man. It's rather boring in the evening.' With this somewhat limited view of the opposite sex, it was perhaps inevitable that he should marry a comparatively simple girl from a working class background, repeating the pattern of his own parents' marriage.

In fact, Renoir didn't marry Aline until 1890, by which time their eldest son, Pierre, was five. All their life together the couple chose a simple lifestyle, even when increasing financial security would have made an alternative a possibility. Renoir also consciously, almost perversely, made no attempt to modify his manners as he mixed with his wealthy patrons. Many of his contemporaries commented on the strong paradox between Renoir's calm, serene paintings, where social and class differences seem to blur into insignificance, and the artist himself, highly strung and restless, often feeling that he belonged to no particular social milieu.

Renoir frequently expressed completely opposite feelings on the

The Cahen D'Anvers Girls, 1881, Collection Museu de Arte de São Paulo, Brazil
(Photo by Luis Hossaka)

same subject. He was known to be the most self-contradictory of men, perhaps a further symptom of his indecisiveness and lack of security. One of the most penetrating studies of the artist's character, particularly in his later years, remains his film director son Jean's affectionate and perceptive tribute, *Renoir, My Father*, published in 1962. In it he writes:

> My father had an almost physical aversion to doing anything he did not wish ... He was like a human sponge, absorbing everything that had to do with life. All that he saw, everything he was aware of became a part of himself. The thought that his every brushtroke gave back these riches a hundred-fold did not occur to him until late in his career. When he took up his brush to paint he always forgot that his work might be of the slightest importance. The role which implies a 'giving' of oneself seemed unrealistic to him.

Renoir saw the world first and foremost as a painter; everything else came second. He was direct and honest about the highly sensual vision of the world which he translated into paint: 'It's with my brush that I make love,' he said, and all his paintings of women, most especially the later ones, seem to bear witness to this. Their intensely feminine charm and sweetness dominate, and he makes no attempt to fathom their individual characters. 'My pictures should make me want to stroll in it, if it is a landscape, or to stroke a breast if it is a figure,' he wrote.

By the time Renoir was sixty he was already suffering from arthritis, which gave him excruciating pain. In 1907, he began sculpting as an alternative. As the arthritis advanced, crippling his fingers, he was obliged to paint with his brushes strapped to his

Bather with Long Hair, Musée de l'Orangerie, Paris

The Dahlias, 1876, The Carnegie Museum of Art, Pittsburgh: Acquired through the generosity of Mrs Alan M. Scaife, 1965

wrists. In 1912 an attack of paralysis restricted him to a wheelchair; some treatment from a Viennese doctor helped him to take a few steps round it, but he did so in terrible pain. 'I give up,' he said, 'If I have to choose between walking and painting, I'd rather paint.'

Renoir constantly stressed that painting should be decorative and optimistic, as he felt there were enough dark and depressing aspects to life. He felt that painting should be an escape from such harsh realities, and on occasion commented with some cynicism on the black view of society depicted by his contemporaries in literature, Zola and Maupassant, or by Manet and Degas in art, himself preferring the more decorative approach of his beloved eighteenth-century Rococco painters. He maintained that it is difficult for painting to be accepted as really great whilst remaining joyful. 'Because Fragonard smiled', he wrote, 'people have quickly said that he is a minor painter. They don't take people seriously who smile.'

Renoir's paintings continue to smile seventy years after his death, giving pleasure to millions. With the onset of old age and severe arthritis, Renoir was deeply disturbed by the changes in the world around him brought about by the horrors of the Great War, in which both his sons were badly wounded. His reaction was typical of him, both as a man and as a painter: he developed an even greater need to escape and create his own world of peace and solace. Consequently, his last great series of paintings, 'The Bathers', became even more of a retreat from an alien age. As was often the case, nobody expressed this better than Renoir himself: 'Each one sings his song if he has the voice.'

Self Portrait
1879

Musée d'Orsay, Paris

This notion of Rousseau's that men are born knowing everything is a literary fancy. We know nothing when we are born. We have all sorts of possibilities in us. But what work it takes to discover them. It took me twenty years to discover painting: twenty years looking at Nature, and above all, going to the Louvre. But when I say discover – ! I am still only just beginning, and I still go on making mistakes ... If you took a peasant from Essoyes, for instance, to hear that masterpiece of all masterpieces, Mozart's *Don Giovanni*, he'd be bored stiff by it. He'd much prefer a popular tune – despite that hypocrite, Jean-Jacques Rousseau. It's simple enough: you begin with a café concert, but you must choose a good one.

Cited in Jean Renoir
Renoir, My Father, 1962

[19]

Le Cabaret de la Mère Anthony
1866

Stockholm National Museum

The 'Cabaret of Mother Antony' is one of my pictures that I remember with most pleasure. It is not that I find the painting itself particularly exciting, but it does remind me of good old Mother Antony and her inn in Marlotte. That was a real village inn! I took the public room, which doubled as a dining room, as the subject of my study. The old woman in a headscarf is Mother Antony herself, and that splendid girl serving drinks is her servant Nana. The white poodle is Toto, who had a wooden leg. I had some of my friends, including Sisley and Le Coeur, pose around the table. The motifs that make up the background were borrowed from scenes painted on the wall; they were unpretentious but often successful paintings by the regulars. I myself drew a sketch of Mürger on the wall and copied it in the upper left-hand corner of the painting.

Cited in Ambrose Vollard
The Life and Work of Renoir, 1919

Spring Bouquet
1866

Fogg Art Museum, Harvard University, Cambridge, Mass
Bequest of Grenville L. Winthrop

I just let my brain rest when I paint flowers ... When I am painting flowers, I establish the tones, I study the values carefully, without worrying about losing the picture. I don't dare to do this with a figure piece for fear of ruining it. The experience which I gain in these works, I eventually apply to my [figure] pictures.

Conversation with Albert André, cited in Albert André
Renoir, 1919

Diana
1867

National Gallery of Art, Washington DC
Chester Dale Collection

I intended to do nothing more than a study of a nude. But the picture was considered pretty improper, so I put a bow in the model's hand and a deer at her feet. I added the skin of an animal to make her nakedness seem less blatant – and the picture became a *Diana!*

Cited in Walter Pach
Renoir, 1950

Skaters in the Bois de Boulogne
1868

Private Collection, USA

People walking and skating in the Bois de Boulogne. I have never been able to stand the cold, and my output of 'winter effects' is limited to this painting and two or three little studies. In any case, even if you can stand the cold, why paint snow? It is one of nature's illnesses.

Cited in Ambrose Vollard
The Life and Work of Renoir, 1919

Monet Painting in his Garden at Argenteuil

1873

Wadsworth Atheneum, Hartford, Connecticutt

I have never had the temperament of a fighter and I should several times have deserted the party if old Monet, who certainly did have it, had not lent me his shoulder for support.

Cited in exhibition catalogue of 'Renoir', Hayward Gallery, 1985

Snowy Landscape

1875

Musée de l'Orangerie, Paris

White does not exist in nature. You admit that you have a sky above that snow. Your sky is blue. That blue must show up in the snow. In the morning there is green and yellow in the sky. These colours must also show up in the snow when you say that you painted your picture in the morning. Had you done it in the evening, red and yellow would have to appear in the snow.

Conversation with a young artist in 1910, cited by John Rewald

Nude in the Sunlight
1875

Musée d'Orsay, Paris

The most simple subjects are eternal . . . The nude woman, whether she emerges from the waves of the sea, or from her own bed, is Venus, or Nini; and one's imagination cannot conceive anything better.

Cited in Jean Renoir
Renoir, My Father, 1962

Ball at the Moulin de la Galette
1876

Musée d'Orsay, Paris

The world knew how to laugh in those days! Machinery had not absorbed all of life: you had leisure for enjoyment and no one was the worse for it.

Cited in Jean Renoir
Renoir, My Father, 1962

Portrait of a Girl, also called The Thought
1876-7

The Barber Institute of Fine Arts, University of Birmingham

Why has such a title been given to my canvas? I wanted to picture a lovely, charming young woman without giving a title which would give rise to the belief that I wished to depict a state of mind of my model ... That girl never thought, she lived like a bird, and nothing more.

Cited in Walter Pach
Renoir, 1950

Madame Charpentier and her Children
1878

Metropolitan Museum of Art, New York

Madame Charpentier's salon was the meeting place of anyone of any importance from the world of politics, literature and the arts. The most frequent visitors to the house were Daudet, Zola, Spuller, the Coquelin brothers, Flaubert, Edmond de Goncourt . . . the portrait by the way by Braquemond of the latter is extremely striking . . .

It was at Madame Charpentier's that I met Juliette Adam, Maupassant and the charming Madame Clapisson whose portrait I painted twice with great enjoyment. Maupassant, I remember was at the height of his fame . . .

I remember also having seen Turgenev at the Charpentiers along with many others whose names I no longer recall . . . I did meet Cézanne there once when he came with Zola, but the gathering was not really to his taste. Whenever we talked about painting in the house, I never failed to say, like Monsieur Choquet, 'Yes, but what about Cézanne?'

Cited in Ambrose Vollard
The Life and Work of Renoir, 1919
Translation by Rachel Barnes

On the Terrace
1879

Art Institute of Chicago

I arrange my subject as I want it, then I go ahead and paint it, like a child. I want a red to be sonorous, to sound like a bell; if it doesn't turn out that way, I add more reds and other colours until I get it. I am no cleverer than that. I have no rules and no methods; anyone can look at my materials or watch how I paint – he will see that I have no secrets. I look at a nude; there are myriads of tiny tints. I must find the ones that will make the flesh on my canvas live and quiver. Nowadays they want to explain everything. But if they could explain a picture, it wouldn't be art. Shall I tell you what I think are the two qualities of art? It must be indescribable and it must be inimitable ... The work of art must seize upon you, wrap you up in itself, carry you away. It is the means by which the artist conveys his passions; it is the current which he puts forth which sweeps you along in his passion.

Cited in Walter Pach
Renoir, 1950

Luncheon of the Boating Party
1880-1

The Phillips Collection, Washington DC

... I am doing a picture of a boating party that I have been itching to do for a long time. I'm not getting any younger and I didn't want to delay this little feast, for later I won't be up to the effort; it's hard enough already ... It's a good thing from time to time to attempt something beyond one's powers.

Letter to Paul Bérard, 1881

Algerian Landscape:
Le Ravin de la Femme Sauvage
1881

Musée d'Orsay, Paris

I wanted to see what the land of sun was like. I am out of luck, for
there is scarcely any at the moment. But it is exquisite all the same,
an extraordinary wealth of nature … I am working a little. I am
going to bring back some figure painting but this is getting more
and more difficult as there are too many painters around.

Letter to Durand-Ruel, 1881

I was glad to see that you were in Algeria, where one feels so far
away yet so near, where the Arab seems like an old comrade whom
one has always known. One mustn't, though, trust this amiable
rogue too much, but it's all very amusing.

Letter to Jeanne Baudot, 1924

The Umbrellas
1881–6

National Gallery, London

About 1883 I had wrung Impressionism dry, and I finally came to
the conclusion that I knew neither how to paint nor how to draw.
In a word, Impressionism was a blind alley, as far as I was
concerned ...
   I finally realized that it was too complicated an affair, a kind of
painting that made you constantly compromise with yourself.
Outdoors there is a greater variety of light than in the studio,
where, to all intents and purposes, it is constant; but, for just that
reason, light plays too great a part outdoors; you have no time to
work out the composition; you can't see what you are doing. I
remember a white wall which reflected on my canvas one day while
I was painting; I keyed down the colour to no purpose – everything
I put on was too light; but, when I took it back to the studio, the
picture looked black ... If the painter works directly from nature,
he ultimately looks for nothing but momentary effects; he does not
try to compose, and soon he gets monotonous.

Cited in Jean Renoir
Renoir, My Father, 1962

[46]

St Mark's Square
1881

Minneapolis Institute of Arts

Some time after returning to Paris, I began planning a trip to Italy.

I went first of all to Venice, where I painted some nudes, a sketch of the Grand Canal, a gondola, the Doge's Palace and St Mark's Square.

I adored Venice – what a marvellous place the Doge's Palace is! That white and pink marble must have looked rather forbidding when it was first built, but it's a stupendous sight after several centuries of sunshine have transformed it to a rich gold.

And St Mark's Basilica! What a welcome change from all those cold Italian Renaissance churches, especially Milan Cathedral with its stupid, dented marble roof which the Italians are so proud of. In St Mark's on the other hand one immediately feels one has entered a very holy place because of this spiritual atmosphere. The mosaics too are magnificent, especially the Christ in Majesty ... Impossible to realize just how beautiful it really all is until you have been there ...

Cited in Ambrose Vollard
The Life and Work of Renoir, 1919
Translation by Rachel Barnes

Le Danse à Bougival
1882

Museum of Fine Arts, Boston

Don't ask me if painting should be objective or subjective – I don't give a damn about such things. It makes me wild to have young painters come to me and ask about the aims of painting. And then there are those who explain to me why I put a red or a blue in such-and-such a place ... Granted that our craft is difficult, complicated; I understand the soul-searchings. But all the same, a little simplicity, a little candour, is necessary.

I just struggle with my figures until they are a harmonious unity with their landscape background, and I want people to feel that neither the setting nor the figures are dull and lifeless.

Cited in Cennino Cennini
Le Livre de l'Art ou Traité de la Peinture translated by V. Mottez
New edition with a letter from Renoir, 1911

Rocky Crags at L'Estaque

1882

Museum of Fine Arts, Boston

How beautiful it is! It's certainly the most beautiful place in the world, and not yet inhabited ... There are only some fishermen and the mountains ... so there are no walls, no properties or few ... here I have the true countryside at my doorstep.

Letter to Paul Bérard, 1882

What lovely landscapes, with distant horizons and the most beautiful colours ... the delicacies of hue are extraordinary ... alas, our poor palette can't match up to it.

Letter to Paul Bérard, 1883

Landscape near Menton
1883

Museum of Fine Arts, Boston

Go and see what others have produced, but never copy anything except Nature. You would be trying to enter into a temperament that is not yours and nothing that you would do would have any character.

Cited in Jean Renoir
Renoir, My Father, 1962

Seated Bather
1883-4

Here one bathes among the rocks which serve as bathing cabins, because there is nothing else; nothing can be prettier than this mixture of women and men crowded together on the rocks. One would think oneself in a Watteau landscape rather than in reality . . . Just as in Athens, the women are not at all afraid of the proximity of men on the nearby rocks. Nothing is more amusing, while one is strolling through these rocks, than surprising young girls getting ready to bathe; even though they are English, they are not particularly shocked.

Letter to Durand-Ruel, Guernsey, 1884

The Return from the Fields
1886

Fitzwilliam Museum, Cambridge

Movement can be as eternal as immobility so long as it is in harmony with nature: if it expresses a natural human function. The flight of a swallow is as eternal as the tranquillity of the 'Seated Scribe' in the Louvre. The statues in the Luxembourg are overactive for intellectual reasons, for literary reasons. A swallow speeds through the air to catch a gnat and to satisfy its hunger: not to verify a principle.

Cited in Walter Pach
Renoir , 1950

The Bathers
1887

Philadelphia Museum of Art
Mr and Mrs Carroll S. Tyson Collection

After three years of experimentation, 'The Bathers', which I considered my masterwork, was finished. I sent it to an exhibition – and what a trouncing I got! This time, everybody, Huysmans in the forefront, agreed that I was really sunk; some even said I was irresponsible. And God knows how I laboured over it!

Cited in Walter Pach
Renoir, 1950

I'm stuck in Paris where I'm getting very fed up, and I'm seeking the perfect model. But I am a figure painter. Alas! sometimes it is great fun, but not when one can only find figures that are not to one's taste.

Letter to Monet, 1884

Washerwomen

1888

Baltimore Museum of Art

I have begun some washerwomen ... I think that it will work out all right this time. It is very soft and coloured, but luminous!

I have taken up again, never to abandon it, my old style, soft and light of touch ... It is quite different from my recent landscapes and from the monotonous portrait of your daughter. It's like the 'Fishergirls' and the 'Woman with a Fan', but with a slight difference caused by a note which I could not find, which I have finally put my hand on. It's nothing new, but rather a follow up to the paintings of the eighteenth century ... This is to give you some idea of my new and last manner of painting (like Fragonard, only not so good) ... I'm not comparing myself, believe me, to an eighteenth-century master. But I must explain the way I am working. Those fellows who give the impression of not painting nature knew more about it than we do.

Letters to Durand-Ruel, 1888

Montagne Sainte-Victoire

1888-91

Yale University Art Gallery

That countryside which I already found so beautiful dazzled me even more. That aridness, with the olive tree which follows the weather – sad in grey weather, resonant in the sun and silvered in the wind ...

Letter to Paul Bérard, 1891

Vines at Cagnes
1908

Brooklyn Museum, New York

The olive tree, what a brute! If you realized how much trouble it has caused me. A tree full of colours. Not great at all. Its little leaves, how they've made me sweat! A gust of wind, and my tree's tonality changes. The colour isn't on the leaves, but in the spaces between them. I know I can't paint nature, but I enjoy struggling with it. A painter can't be great if he doesn't understand landscape. Landscape, in the past, has been a term of contempt, particularly in the eighteenth century; but still, that century that I adore did produce some landscapists. I'm one with the eighteenth century. With all modesty, I consider not only that my art descends from a Watteau, a Fragonard, a Hubert Robert, but also that I am one with them.

Letter to Réné Gimpel, 1918

The Clown

1909

Musée de l'Orangerie, Paris

The costume was completed with white stockings which I obstinately refused to put on. My father demanded the stockings in order to finish the picture, but he could do nothing: they pricked me. So my mother brought some silk stockings; they tickled me. Threats followed, and then negotiations; one after the other I was promised a spanking, an electric railway, being sent to a boarding school, and a box of oil colours. Finally I agreed to put on cotton stockings for a few moments; my father, holding back a rage which was ready to burst out, finished the picture despite the contortions I was making to scratch myself. The railway and the box of colours rewarded so much effort.

Claude Renoir
'Souvenir sur mon Père' in
Seize Aquarelles et Sanguinés de Renoir, 1948

Gabrielle à La Rose
1911

Musée d'Orsay, Paris

Happy painting which, very late in life, still gives you illusions and sometimes joy.

Painting is done to decorate walls. So it should be as rich as possible. For me a picture – for we are forced to paint easel pictures – should be something likeable, joyous and pretty – yes, pretty. There are enough ugly things in life for us not to add to them. I well realize that it is difficult for painting to be accepted as really great painting whilst remaining joyous. Because Fragonard smiled, people have quickly said that he is a minor painter. They don't take people seriously who smile.

Cited in Albert André
Renoir, 1919

Seated Nude
1916

I have been told many times that I ought not to like Boucher, because he is 'only a decorator.' As if being a decorator made any difference! Why, Boucher is one of the painters who best understood the female body. What fresh, youthful buttocks he painted, with the most enchanting little dimples! It's odd that people are never willing to give a man credit for what he can do. They say: 'I like Titian better than Boucher.' Good Lord, so do I! But that has nothing to do with the fact that Boucher painted lovely women superbly. A painter who has the feel for breasts and buttocks is saved!

Cited in Jean Renoir
Renoir, My Father, 1962

Bathers
1918-19

Musée d'Orsay, Paris

God's best works . . . this supreme achievement . . .
   The pain passes . . . but the beauty remains. I'm quite happy, and
I shall not die until I have completed my master work. Yesterday I
thought it was finished, that I could not put on another brushstroke
to better it, but *la nuit porte conseil*; and now I see that three or four
days' more work on it will give it a deeper touch.

Cited in Frank Harris
*Henri Matisse and Renoir, Master Painters in
Contemporary Portraits*, 1924

Self Portrait
1910

Collection Durand-Ruel

When I look back at my life I compare it to one of those corks thrown into the river. Off it goes, then it is drawn into an eddy, pulled back, plunges and rises, is caught by a grass, makes desperate efforts to get free and ends by losing itself, I do not know where ...

When I look at the old masters I feel a simple little man, yet I believe that among my works there will be enough to assure me a place in the French School, that school which I love so much, which is so pretty, so clear, such good company. And with nothing rowdy about it ...

Cited in Jean Renoir
Renoir, My Father, 1962

[77]

CHRONOLOGY

Pierre-Auguste Renoir
1841-1919

1841   Born in Limoges on 25 February, one of five sons of a poor tailor.

1845   Family moves to Paris where Renoir attends local school.

1854   Apprenticed to porcelain factory. Paints ceramics in Rococo style.

1862   Meets Monet, Sisley and Bazille at Gleyre's studio.

1863   Leaves Gleyre's studio and studies at the Louvre with Fantin-Latour.

1866   Paints with Monet in Paris.
Paints 'Le Cabaret de la Mère Anthony' in Marlotte, which is subsequently rejected by the Salon.

1869   Paints with Monet at Bougival; both painters do views of La Grenouillère.

1872   Sets up a studio in Paris and visits Monet in Argenteuil.
Paints views of Paris and meets Theodore Duret. It is at this time that Impressionism is formed.

1874   First Impressionist exhibition, where Renoir exhibits seven paintings.

1876 Second Impressionist exhibition, where Renoir exhibits fifteen paintings.

1880 Paints 'The Luncheon of the Boating Party'. Begins to have doubts about the future of Impressionism.

1881 Begins to make trips to warmer climates, visiting Algeria, Italy and the South of France. The influence of the Renaissance painters, especially Raphael, begins to change his work. Also visits Rome, Florence and Venice.

1883 Visits Cézanne in L'Estaque.

1884 By this time, Renoir no longer paints as a strict Impressionist.

1885 Birth of his son Pierre.

1888 Following onset of arthritis, spends the colder months at Cagnes.

1890 Marries Aline Charigot and they recognize Pierre as their legitimate child.

1906 Settles permanently at Cagnes. As arthritis gets worse, he begins to dictate sculpture to an assistant.

1917 Matisse visits Renoir for the first time at Cagnes. They see each other regularly and Renoir becomes sympathetic to Fauvism.

1919 Dies on 3 December in Cagnes at the age of seventy-eight.

ACKNOWLEDGEMENTS

The editor and publishers would like to thank the following for their help in providing the photographs of paintings reproduced in this book:

Art Institute of Chicago (pp41, 73)
Baltimore Museum of Art (p63)
Barber Institute of Fine Arts, University of Birmingham (p37)
Bridgeman Art Library (p27)
Brooklyn Museum, New York (p67)
Carnegie Museum of Art, Pittsburgh (p16)
Durand-Ruel & CIE, Paris (pp7, 11, 77)
Fine Arts Museum of San Francisco (p10)
Fitzwilliam Museum, Cambridge (p59)
Fogg Art Museum, Harvard University, Cambridge, Mass (pp23, 57)
Metropolitan Museum of Art, New York (p39)
Minneapolis Institute of Arts (p49)
Museu de Arte de São Paulo, Brazil (p13)
Museum of Fine Arts, Boston (pp51, 53, 55)
National Gallery, London (p47)
National Gallery of Art, Washington DC (p25)
Philadelphia Museum of Art (pp9, 61)
The Phillips Collection, Washington DC (p43)
Photo RMN (cover, frontispiece, pp15, 19, 31, 33, 35, 45, 69, 71, 75)
Stockholm National Museum (p21)
Wadsworth Atheneum, Hartford, Connecticutt (p29)
Yale University Art Gallery (p65)

We would also like to thank the publishers of the following books for access to the material contained in them which has been reproduced in this volume:

Renoir, His Life, Art and Letters B. E. White New York 1984
'Renoir' Hayward Gallery 1985
Renoir Walter Pach 1950
Renoir, My Father Jean Renoir 1962
The Life and Work of Renoir Ambrose Vollard 1919
Le Livre de l'Art ou Traité de la Peinture Cennino Cennini translated by V. Mottez, new edition with a letter from Renoir 1911
'Souvenir sur mon Père' Claude Renoir in *Seize Aquarelles et Sanguinés de Renoir* 1948
Renoir Albert André 1919
Henri Matisse and Renoir, Master Painters in Contemporary Portraits Frank Harris 1924

Every effort has been made to contact the owners of the copyright of all the information contained in this book, but if, for any reason, any acknowledgements have been omitted, the publishers ask those concerned to contact them.

759.4   Barnes, Rachel.
BAR
        Artists by
          themselves.

                                    012554
$16.45

DATE			

© THE BAKER & TAYLOR CO.